Quick & Easy

Beading

Quick & Easy

Beading

15 step-by-step projects—simple to make, stunning results

ROBIN BELLINGHAM,
HANA GLOVER & JEMA HEWITT

CRE**A**TIVE
ARTS & CRAFTS™

An imprint of **CREATIVE HOMEOWNER**, Upper Saddle River, NJ

First published in the United States and Canada in 2004 by

CREATIVE
ARTS & CRAFTS

An imprint of Creative Homeowner®
Upper Saddle River, NJ
Creative Homeowner® is a registered trademark of Federal Marketing Corp.

Current printing (last digit) 10 9 8 7 6 5 4 3 2 1
Library of Congress card number: 2004101633
ISBN: 1-58011-201-3

Senior Editor: Clare Sayer
Production: Hazel Kirkman
Design: AG&G Books Glyn Bridgewater
Photographer: Shona Wood
Editorial Direction: Rosemary Wilkinson

Reproduction by Pica Digital of Pte Ltd, Singapore
Printed and bound in Malaysia

Acknowledgments

Hana would like to thank Richard for helping us start The Bead Shop in the first place. Sarah for all her support. Becca and Dave for testing the projects. Hannah in Oz for all the help and inspiration she has given. Last and not least all the staff at The Bead Shop (Jo, Rosie, Jema, Jenette, Angela, Becky, and Sophie) for all of their hard work in helping us keep to our business plan and grow the shop to what it is today because without it we would never have been approached to do this book.

Jema would like to thank Lynn Hardy for her support and enthusiasm and for first tempting me with beads and teaching me the beading stitches! Nik Hewitt—my wonderful husband for happily putting up with beads EVERYWHERE and showing me how to use a computer. My Mum and Dad for always having loads of exciting creative oddments lying about, and encouraging me to play with them.

Robin would like to thank Jill—Mum, this is for you to show all those to whom you may have been embarrassed to admit that one of your sons makes a living from beads. Thanks for never getting in the way of whatever I've wanted to do.

CREATIVE HOMEOWNER

A division of Federal Marketing Corp.
24 Park Way
Upper Saddle River, NJ 07458
www.creativehomeowner.com

Contents

 Projects

Introduction

Beads have been in use for 40,000 years, originally a part of religious rites and ceremonies, and as currency up until the colonization of the Americas. Today you can use beads to create a stunning item of jewelry to complement any outfit or to present as a fantastic personal gift. A simple design can take just two hours to complete, or a more absorbing project may take many evenings to finish. Whichever it is, the results are sure to be spectacular.

The projects included in this book have been graded in terms of difficulty, from simple to more complicated, but each one can stand on its own. You may wish to go through the projects one by one or pick out particular ones that catch your eye. Either way, you'll enjoy the whole creative process.

Once you have started to experiment with beads, your knowledge of this craft will grow, along with your collection of beads, very rapidly. Don't be afraid to buy beads just because you like the way they look, even if you are not sure what you are going to do with them. The ideas will come to you, especially at unlikely times, and it's always useful to have a good selection of beads at hand for when you are inspired.

We hope you have fun with the ideas and projects in this book and experiment with them to your own specifications. The same project can look very different when you use beads of different shapes, sizes, and colors. Use your creativity, and don't forget that there is no wrong way to go with beads.

Materials

There is a fantastic range of beads to be found, along with a number of speciality threads for arranging them and jewelry findings to finish a piece. If you don't have a bead shop or quality craft store in your area, don't worry. Everything you need can be bought from a catalog or on the Internet.

Beads

Beads are available in so many different colors, shapes, and sizes that it is often difficult to know where to start when choosing them. For the projects in this book, we have given guidance as to the type of beads you will need and the quantities where appropriate. But you are much more likely to buy beads in pre-packed quantities rather than in specific numbers. Don't worry if you can't find exactly the same size or color that we have used. Many of the projects can be made up with your own choice of beads.

Antique beads are stunning one-of-a-kind art pieces, but so are many modern beads. From hand-rolled felt beads and hand-carved semiprecious to iridescent dichroic lamp-worked one-of-a-kind beads, some simply cannot be mass-produced. One gorgeous handmade bead can create a perfect focus for a necklace, as well as becoming an heirloom in its own right in years to come. Look out for local artists as well as exciting finds while traveling abroad.

Bali beads are traditionally handmade sterling-silver beads with intricate designs created on the bead surface using sterling silver wire.

Bugle beads are long, cylindrical beads, the tubular version of seed beads. They are available in much the same colors and finishes as seed beads, with sizes ranging from $1/15-1^1/4$ inches in length. Bugles can be round or hexagonal in shape. Twisted bugles are formed by twisting the hexagonal tubes while the glass is molten and before they are cut into bugles.

Crystal beads and bicones are available in myriad colors and finishes, the most popular being the AB, or Aurora Borealis, finish. Crystal beads are machine-cut to produce sparkling facets. They are available in a tremendous range of shapes including bicone, round, and cube. I find the bicone the most versatile crystal shape to use. Crystal pendants are also available in shapes such as crosses, drops, and hearts.

Delica or Treasure Beads are the trade names for precision-made Japanese cylindrical seed beads. They have relatively large holes and are consistent in size and shape so they fit together perfectly when woven. This makes them ideal for bead weaving.

Kiln-made glass beads are produced by winding heated glass that is not quite molten around a steel rod then pressing it in a metal mold to form the shape. Indian glass beads are often characterized by a chalky residue that is inside the hole. This is caused by a thin layer of clay that is used on the steel rod to prevent the bead from sticking. Indian glass beads are mostly handmade in workshops.

Natural beads, such as shells, are available on a beach, as are other natural sources such as seeds and acorns. Be careful not to break them when making a hole for threading. This is the only drawback to using these "free" beads. Bone is another material that is popular for making beads. Usually made from cattle bone, these beads can be carved, painted, or dyed.

Pearls are nature's classic gems, created by the humble oyster. Natural pearls are extremely rare, and most real pearls are now cultivated. Many shapes are available, from the affordable tiny rice grain and irregular baroque, to the very expensive perfect round pearl. Assorted colors are also found naturally, including the famous black pearl. Others can be dyed. Wonderful fake pearl beads are also available in varying degrees of quality and realism, but the real thing is always obvious.

Plastic beads are available in a much larger range of colors and effects than any other type of bead. They include glow-in-the-dark and neon, which are inexpensive and fun to use. Most plastic beads are produced in the USA or China.

Polymer clay is a wonderfully versatile medium for creating beads and pendants. It is soft, like natural clay, until it is baked in an ordinary oven. Although polymer clay is a relatively new medium, many wonderful artists are constantly inventing new techniques for making beads and pendants with it. Incredible effects can be achieved, from millefiori to faux semiprecious stones, with very little needed in the way of special equipment.

Pressed-glass beads are formed from molten glass pressed between two molds. Adding oxides to the glass before it is pressed creates the colors. Pressed-glass beads come in many shapes, such as cubes, ovals, flowers, and leaves. Pressed faceted beads are an inexpensive alternative to cut-glass or crystal beads. The many colors and finishes available, such as frosted and Aurora Borealis (AB), make these a very popular type of bead.

Seed beads, also known as *rocailles*, are tiny round glass beads. They are available in a range of numbered sizes—confusingly, the higher the number the smaller the bead. The size is often written as 10/0 or 10°. Sizes between 15 (tiny) and 5 (large) are readily available. The most commonly used sizes are 10 and 11. Seed beads can be found in a huge variety of colors and finishes, and are manufactured in different shapes, such as cylinders, hexagons, and triangles. They are produced mainly in the Czech Republic and Japan, with lower-quality versions also made in China and India. Czech seed beads tend to be round, and Japanese seed beads have large holes and are more cylindrical and consistent in shape.

Semiprecious beads such as amethyst, garnet, lapis lazuli, and turquoise are very beautiful and add value to a special piece of jewelry. Many stones are available both as round beads, carved, and faceted shapes, as well as the irregular tumbled chips. Some stones are marked out as birthstones while others are alleged to impart good fortune or feelings to their owners, which can add meaning to a present.

Venetian beads are handmade glass beads created by "lamp work." A glass rod is formed into a bead and worked over a special torch. The beads are created in layers and exquisitely decorated. Venice has been a center for glass bead makers since Renaissance times. Techniques for making and working glass were shrouded in mystery and the secrets of the Italian craftsmen were kept for hundreds of years.

Wooden beads are a popular choice. Wood is incredibly versatile because it can be carved, varnished, or stained. Beads can be made from many different types of wood, each of which has a natural beauty that is often enhanced by a simple coat of varnish. Wooden beads are available in many shapes, sizes, and bright colors.

Threads and wires

The material you thread your beads on depends on the type of project you are creating. There are a whole range of options available.

Beading thread is a very strong polyester thread that is primarily used to hang semiprecious beads and stones. This is because of the weight of the beads, and because older and lower-quality semiprecious beads tend to have sharp edges around the hole, which can wear some thread very quickly. Beading thread is found in a few colors and from sizes 27-gauge to 21-gauge. It must be cut with scissors.

Chains will transform a simple pendant into something really special, so it's worth keeping a few in your workbox for emergency presents. Chains are available in gold, silver, and base metals, and are created by attaching links in various ways. Chain can also be measured off the roll for special projects.

Cotton strands are often plaited together to make a strong string for large-holed beads. It is sometimes referred to as bootlace.

Elastic cord was originally used in the clothing industry, but it was soon discovered by beaders as it is incredibly versatile and easy to use. As it expands to several times its original length, no clasp is required. Just tie a couple of knots, you may even be able to hide the knot inside a bead. The fabric elastic has a rubber core and is now available in a few colors, other than black and white, and a limited number of gauges. Thinner plastic elastic is now widely available in lots of colors, including clear. Although not as strong as the fabric elastic, this elastic is suitable for seed beads and other small-holed beads. It requires at least three knots to secure it properly, and a dab of glue will always help.

Leather cord is available in similar gauges to cotton strand but not such a variety of colors. Leather tends to be weaker than cotton bootlace and can be snapped with your hands. There are plenty of different threads available for stringing beads—the bead-hole size will dictate which you can and cannot use. Experiment and see which one you prefer.

Memory wire is used in all sorts of projects. It is very strong, hard wire that always reverts back to its original round shape, hence its name. It is available in a range of sizes. It needs to be cut with speciality pliers to however many coils are needed. The sharp ends can then be made into a loop or a bead cap glued in place and beads threaded on.

smaller gauges are not suitable for stringing beads, but the larger gauges can be used to make choker bands or tiara bases.

Tigertail is a very fine, plastic-coated metal cord. It is available in a range of colors and an assortment of stranded widths. Because of its metal core it is extremely tough, but it doesn't kink in the same way that wire does. Some softer brands can be knotted and manipulated like thread; others are stiffer and need crimps to fasten on necklace ends.

Waxed thread is slightly thicker than nylon and available in brighter colors. It is also ideal for bead weaving.

Jewelry findings

Findings are an important part of any jewelry project, and there are a number of options available.

Clasps are the finishing touch on a piece, from elaborate to simple, each has its place. Simple screw-together torpedo-and-barrel clasps are great on necklaces but difficult to manage one-handed on a bracelet. Lobster clasps and bolt rings are very easy to use, with a jump ring as a loop for the other side. Special clasps are available for multi-stranded projects. It's always worth keeping some gold and sterling-silver clasps on hand for extra special designs.

Crimps are available in a variety of types, but the most common are tiny, metal, circular beads that are crushed against threads with pliers for securing. The crimp grips the thread and doesn't move. Tubular crimps tend to be neater when crushed and are a lot less likely to break the thread. Crimps can also be used to space beads on a strand that can't be

Monofilament is a plastic unstranded thread, like nylon fishing wire. It is very strong and is often used in Japanese-style bead-weaving crystal projects or "floating" necklaces. It is available in an assortment of widths and is usually transparent or black. Although it is not stretchy, it does have a bit of give, so it is unsuitable for heavy beads that are threaded in a simple strand.

Nylon is a strong but very thin thread originally used in the manufacture of clothing and upholstery coverings. As a thin, strong thread, it was adopted by the beading world because it is ideal for projects that involve passing through beads several times, or passing through very small beads like Delicas. The most popular and widely available size is D. Other gauges are

available and the choice of colors is excellent.

Pearl threads are manmade fibers used for threading pearls. Traditionally pearls were threaded on pure silk strands to preserve their luster. Speciality pearl cord is silky, which makes it easy to create and manipulate knots in. Some cords even have needles ready threaded in the pack. Pearls are knotted to protect them from scratching or chipping each other, but an added bonus is that if the cord breaks you don't lose the whole precious strand.

Plated wires usually have a copper core that has been plated either silver or gold. The most frequently used diameters range from 32-gauge through to 14-gauge. This kind of wire is used for handmade jewelry findings and link chains. The

knotted. Simply slide the crimp onto the thread and crush with a pair of needle-nose pliers. Use crimps on either side of a bead to stop it from moving on the thread and to space the bead from its neighbor. Crimps can also be used as a spacer bead, either on threads or an earring pin. They are also used at the end of a thread to attach a clasp.

Earring wires can be found in a range of shapes. Some look like a simple fish-hook or kidney wire, while others have a post-and-butterfly back. Different front fittings take dangles or glue-on cabochons. When making earrings as gifts for friends, remember that some people are allergic to base metal and can only wear gold or silver.

Headpins and eye pins are used for the majority of earring projects. The headpin has a flat end, which stops the beads from falling off the pin. The eye pin has a loop, which also stops beads from falling off the pin but gives you the advantage of either hanging another pin from the loop, making long earrings, or hanging a pendant below the beads. Both types of pin need a loop at the top so that they can be hung from an earring wire.

Jump rings are a circular piece of small-gauge wire, which has a break in the loop so it can be twisted open. Jump rings are useful items to have on hand as they can change the orientation of a pendant or be used to link two closed loops together. Several jump rings together make an ideal safety chain for awkward clasps. Several diameters and shapes are available. Jump rings can also be handmade using

plated wire and a pair of round-nose pliers.

Necklace ends are used to attach a clasp to the necklace cord. They are also sometimes called calottes or clamshells. Necklace ends can be side or end opening. The side openers have the thread entering from the side, whereas the end openers have the thread entering through the center of the necklace end. These findings are used on smaller gauges of beadstring and can be attached by either tying a knot in the thread or using a crimp.

Spacer bars are essential for multi-stranded projects, because they keep the different layers separate and are threaded on as part of the design. Most common are those with three or five holes, but other sizes are available too. They can be found in gold and sterling silver as well as

plated metals. You can even find fabulous fancy ones to use as a central feature of the design.

Thong ends are used for larger gauges of thread, usually $2/5$ inch or larger. They work by inserting the thread into the end and crushing the last coil against itself, securing the thread by crimping. They are usually available as plated items. There is a loop at the end, which connects with the clasp. Thin cord is better secured when doubled over.

Triangular clamps are used when circular jump rings will not fit. This is generally when a hole is not close enough to the edge of the pendant or the pendant is especially wide. These clamps are better when hanging crystal pendants. They are open when you buy them, and when positioned correctly, just need the legs pushing towards each other to grip.

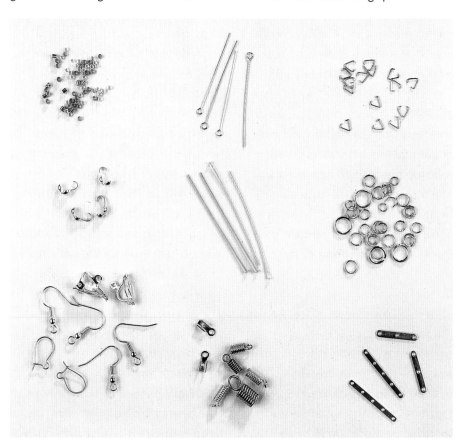

Tools

To get started with any beadwork project, you will need a few basic tools. You may already have some of them around the house or garage, but you may need to buy other, special equipment. The following is a list of all of the equipment you are likely to need when making the projects in this book.

Bead design board

Bead design boards come in either a single or multi-strand configuration. Shallow channels in the board allow you to lay out the beads in a chosen pattern without having to re-thread them repeatedly to see how the design looks. The channels stop rounded beads from moving out of line, making the pattern easy to see. Most boards have semicircular channels and a unit of measure around the outer side to help you to determine the length of your project.

Bead tray and mat

One useful piece of equipment for the beader is a tray and mat. The mat will stop the beads from rolling away. The tray allows you to keep all of your beads and tools close at hand, and is a useful way to store and carry your work without disrupting it.

Glue

Glue is used to space beads along a thread. Other uses include stiffening or preventing fraying at the end of a thread, making threading without a needle easier, and securing knots so that they cannot come undone when you least expect it. Fabric glues are good for porous threads, whereas cyanoacrylate glue can be used on all threads, although it tends to be brittle and less controllable. We use special bead glue, available from most bead suppliers, because it has slightly better results.

Needles

Needles are an important tool when it comes to beadwork and it is a good idea to keep a selection in your workbox. Flexible beading needles are made from twisted wire and have a large, easily threaded eye that compresses to get through small beads. For bead weaving and embroidery, a sharp beading needle is best. It is like a normal sewing needle but much thinner. The eye is also thinner so a needle threader can be invaluable. For thick cord, try stiffening the end with tape or a dab of superglue.

Pliers

There are a variety of jewelry pliers available on the market. Some of them are specific tools for specific beading tasks. Round-nose pliers—both plier jaws are round—are used to make loops and spirals. Flat-nose pliers—both jaws are flat and, more importantly, smooth—are used for gripping and crimping. Some pliers come with a serrated surface. This does help with gripping but it can also mark and damage your work.

Reamer

Reamers have several attachments to enable you to clear or enlarge holes

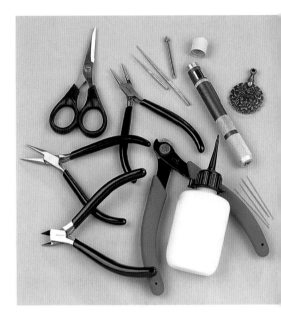

in beads. Another attachment will smooth sharp edges where the thread enters and exits the bead. It is mostly used with semiprecious beads, ceramics, or glass.

Scissors and thread cutters

A small pair of very sharp embroidery scissors is invaluable. Only use them for thread, never paper or wire, which will blunt them. Thread cutters are wonderful gadgets and are the only cutters allowed on airlines (but you should check on this). A circular blade is completely encased in a decorative metal cover with tiny sections cut away, for a safe trimmer.

Wire cutters

Do not use scissors to cut wire or they will be ruined. Use wire cutters for all wire except memory wire, which is extremely strong and will wreck normal cutters very quickly. Special memory wire cutters are available.

Techniques

Beadwork does not involve a lot of complicated techniques, but there are a few basic skills you will need to learn. Although the projects have full step-by-step instructions, it is worth taking the time to familiarize yourself with the basics.

Necklace ends

Necklace ends all work in the same way—by covering a crimp or knot securing the necklace end to the thread. These findings are either side closing, end closing, or cupped.

To use a side-closing necklace end

1 Tie a knot or crimp with flat-nose pliers as close as possible to the last bead on the project.
2 Using the pliers, sit the knot or crimp in one cup and close the second cup onto the first.
3 Hook the metal tail of the necklace end onto a clasp and loop it back on itself. Repeat at the other end.

To use an end-closing necklace end

1 Thread the strand through the hole where the two cups of the necklace end fold. Crush a crimp bead with flat-nose pliers or tie a knot in the thread.

2 Use flat-nose pliers to close the two cups together, completely covering the crimp or knot.

3 Hook the metal tail of the necklace end onto a clasp and loop it back on itself. Repeat for the other end but fully open the necklace end so that the crimp or knot can be secured close to the necklace end and bead.

To use a cupped necklace end

1 Thread the strand(s) through the hole at the bottom of the necklace end cup.
2 Crush a crimp bead with flat-nose pliers or tie a knot in the thread.
3 Hook the metal tail of the necklace end onto a clasp and loop it back on itself. For the second end, use pliers to crimp or to move and tighten the knot as close as possible to the necklace end.

Opening and closing jump rings

It is best to open and close a jump ring using two pairs of pliers.
1 Locate the split in the ring where the two ends meet. Holding each side with the two pairs of pliers, pull

one side toward you and push the other side away from you.

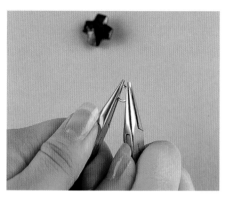

2 Connect the jump ring and repeat Step 1 in reverse. This opens and closes the jump ring without deforming the shape.

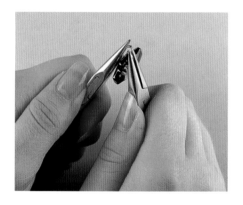

Making a headpin loop

Headpins are used to hang beads and for making pendants. They are also especially useful for making earrings.
1 Hold the headpin with round-nose pliers, leaving a tail at the top of at least $\frac{1}{2}$ inch. Twist your hand and the pliers to bend the headpin so that, looking straight on, it looks like 10 to 6 on a clock face. Here you'll notice that one jaw is on top. Smooth the tail back around the top jaw so that the tail is pointing down the same way as the main body.

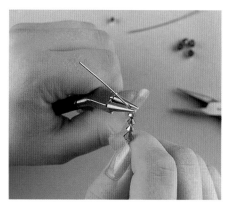

2 Release your grip on the pin with the pliers and rotate until one jaw is above and one is inside the part-made loop. Continue to smooth the tail completely around the jaw in the middle of the loop so it crosses the main body of the pin. Remove the headpin from the pliers.

3 Holding onto the tail—the piece you are cutting off—rest the wire cutters on the shoulder formed in Step 1. Snip off the tail with the wire cutters.

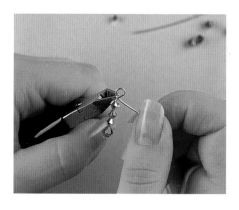

Couching beads onto fabric

1 You will need two sharp needles on two separate lengths of thread. Tie a knot in the first length of thread and bring it up through the fabric where you want the beadwork to begin. Pick up the beads with the needle. Bring up the second needle and thread between the first and second beads.

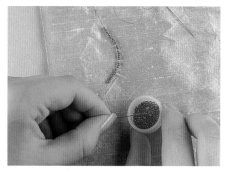

2 With the second needle and thread, start sewing down every third or fourth bead by passing the needle over the beads.

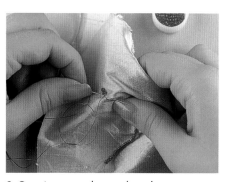

3 Continue to the end and secure both threads neatly to finish.

Beaded backstitch

1 Knot the end of a piece of thread and, using a sharp beading needle, bring the needle up through the fabric. Place a bead on the needle and push down to the fabric.

2 Make a backstitch by bringing the point of the needle up where you want the next bead to be. Add a bead and repeat the backstitch.

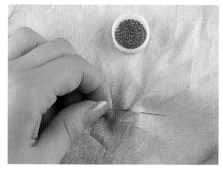

3 You can place the beads as close or far apart as you wish. This stitch can be used with all beads from seed to bugles for various effects.

Fringing

1 Thread a sharp beading needle with plenty of thread and attach it firmly to the fabric with a few running stitches. Thread on the required number of beads to make the fringe the correct length.

2 Thread a small round bead onto the end of the fringe (this acts as the "turning bead") and pass the needle back up through the fringe.

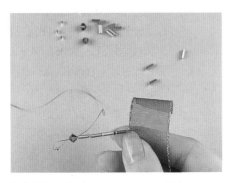

3 Add a stitch at the top and then make a running stitch along the fabric to where you want to position the next fringe. Repeat from Step 1.

Peyote stitch

Peyote stitch is very versatile and can be used to make a whole range of items, such as the choker on pages 38-41. Peyote stitch can be created as even or odd count and flat or in a tube. These instructions are for flat, even-count peyote.

1 Thread a sharp beading needle with a length of thin nylon thread. Place a stopper bead on the end of the thread by looping back through the bead. This stops your beads from falling off the end of the thread and is removed when the project is finished. It is best to use a different colored bead to avoid confusion. Using the needle to pick them up, thread on an even number of beads. Peyote stitch is best worked in two colors (A and B) so that you can see the rows building up. Thread away from the stopper.

2 For the second row, pick up a bead —the same color as the last bead on the first row (A)—and pass the needle back through the next-to-last bead. Pick up another bead in the same color, skip a bead, and pass the needle through the next bead. Continue all the way down the end of the row, skipping every other bead. You should now be working back towards the stopper bead. Add a third row by picking up a bead (B), skipping the next bead and passing the needle once more through the odd-numbered bead. Repeat all the way down the row.

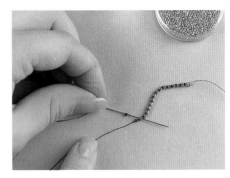

3 For the fourth row, pick up a bead (A) and pass the needle through the bead that sticks out. Repeat up the row, making sure the tension is firm.

Adding extra thread

Adding extra thread is only necessary when you will need a particularly large amount of it, such as with peyote stitch. For all other projects, start with enough thread.

1 Leave a tail of the first thread and thread the needle with the second thread. Starting a little way back through the weaving, thread the needle through the pattern a second time, ensuring that you can still see the tail—you can snip this off later.

2 Work your way through the last few beads in the pattern to get to the point where you stopped. Pull on the new thread to see if there is enough tension holding it in the weave. If not, pull the thread through and start again a little further back.

Making a spiral rope

Spiral rope is a form of bead weaving that creates a chain, which can be made to any length. It is ideal for making necklaces and bracelets.

1 Thread a sharp beading needle with a length of thin nylon thread. Place a stopper bead (to stop your bead falling off) on the end of the thread by looping back through the bead. Thread on four size 10 seed beads for the core, then three more in a contrasting color. Thread the needle back up through the four core beads.

2 Thread on one core bead and three outsiders—in the contrasting color. Pass the needle up through the top four core beads, leaving out the bottom one.

3 Repeat Step 2, making sure the outside beads are either to the right or the left of the previous row. Otherwise, the rope will not "spiral" properly.

Using a bead loom

Bead-loom weaving is a quick and easy way of weaving beads to make a flat strip. The beads are arranged in straight rows, and the design can be worked out on a grid in advance. If you want to create your own designs use the grid on page 79.

1 Count the number of beads across the design and add one. This will be the number of warp thread. Measure out the number of threads to your required length with an additional 1 foot on each. You will need one more thread than the number of beads per row. Knot them together at one end. Hook the knot over the nail (anchor) at one end of the loom. Wrap the thread around the spool and tighten the nut.

2 Separate the threads on the spring so that each is in a separate groove, next to the previous one.

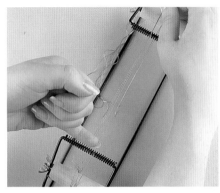

3 Tie the other ends of the thread together and repeat the process on the other end of the loom. Make sure the threads do not cross over and that they are taut. These are the warp threads.

4 When you have finished the weaving, release one end of your work at a time. Start by pairing up the threads and tying a simple knot in each pair. Pull the knot so that it moves down the two strands and sits next to the bead to keep the tension. If you have an odd number of threads, tie three strands together.

5 Using a flexible beading needle, thread all strands to the required length, before adding a clasp. Or, plait the strands together before adding a clasp. Repeat at the other side of your work.

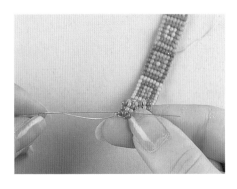

Crystal stretch bracelet

HANA GLOVER

Crystal beads make fantastic sparkly bracelets, and when threaded onto elastic, no clasp is needed. I am always experimenting to find new ways to use crystal cubes—they're such a fascinating shape. This bracelet is stunning, but very easy to make.

As well as looking good, the seed beads on either side protect the elastic from the edges of the cubes, which can be sharp.

You will need

Materials

- 60 ⅙-inch crystal AB faceted beads
- 5-foot length of 25-gauge elastic beading cord
- 60 size 8 or 9 crystal AB seed beads
- 30 ⅙-inch fuchsia crystal cubes
- 2 tubular crimps

Tools

- Masking tape (optional)
- Scissors
- Flat-nose pliers

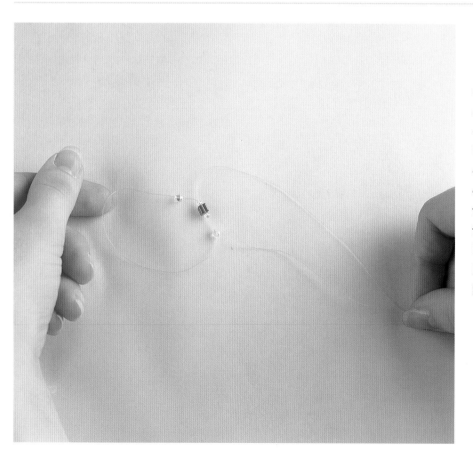

1 Thread two ⅙-inch crystal AB beads onto 5 feet of elastic beading cord. Now thread on one crystal seed bead, one crystal cube, and another seed bead. Take the other end of the elastic and thread it back through the seed bead, cube, and seed-bead group in the opposite direction. Pull the ends of the elastic to move the beads down towards the bottom of the thread, leaving a 4-inch loop. The loop can be taped to the work surface to keep it in place.

★☆☆ **Skill level**   🕐 **1–2 hours**

2 Thread another ⅙-inch AB bead onto each end of the elastic. As before, thread a seed, a cube, then another seed onto one end of the elastic, then thread the other end back through in the opposite direction. Pull the ends of the elastic to move the beads down to join the first set.

3 Continue adding groups of ⅙-inch AB, seed, cube, and seed in the same fashion until the bracelet has approximately 28 cube beads.

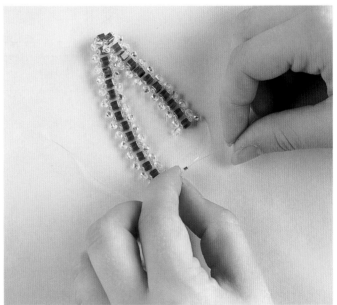

4 Thread a tubular crimp onto each end of the elastic. Cut the tail loop of elastic formed in Step 1. Thread each new end through the crimp on the other end of the bracelet. (Thread through the corresponding crimp bead so that the bracelet doesn't have a twist in it.)

5 Pull the ends of the elastic tight, and crush the crimp bead with a pair of flat-nose pliers. Repeat on the other side and trim the excess elastic.

Helpful hint
Tubular crimps are smooth and less likely to shear the elastic when crushed.

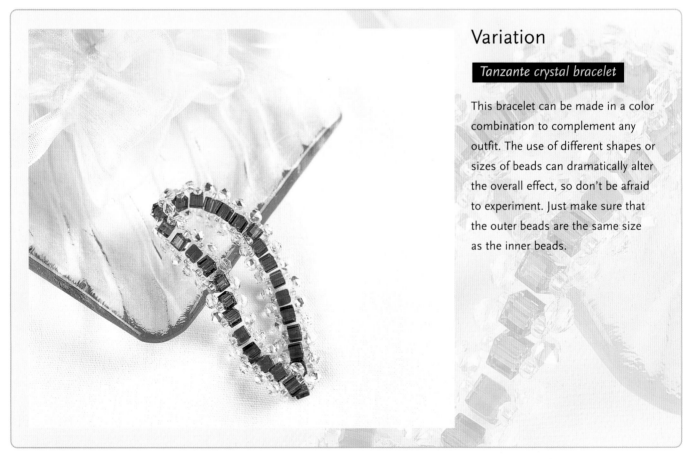

Variation

Tanzante crystal bracelet

This bracelet can be made in a color combination to complement any outfit. The use of different shapes or sizes of beads can dramatically alter the overall effect, so don't be afraid to experiment. Just make sure that the outer beads are the same size as the inner beads.

Semiprecious stone earrings

ROBIN BELLINGHAM

Semiprecious stone chips, or tumbled chips, are great beads to use because their irregular shape gives the finished project an individuality that cannot be reproduced exactly. These earrings feature mother-of-pearl, which is believed to promote wealth, and rose quartz, believed to promote love.

These simple earrings are great for beginners and make unique gifts, because no two pairs will be the same.

You will need

Materials

- 8 6-inch lengths of 22-gauge silver-plated wire (more if required)
- Rose quartz and mother-of-pearl semiprecious tumbled chips (about 12 of each color)
- 2 sterling-silver fishhooks

Tools

- Round-nose pliers
- Flat-nose pliers
- Wire cutters

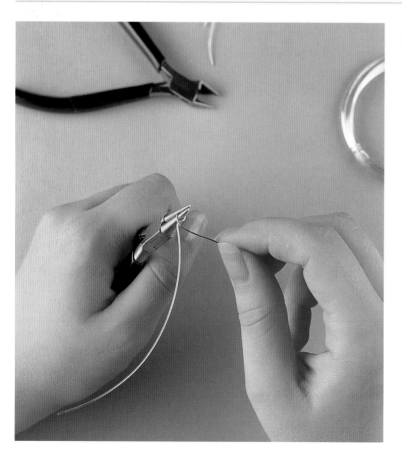

1 Take one 6-inch length of 22-gauge wire. Grip the wire with round-nose pliers about 2 inches from one end. The wire is now divided into two sections—a long stem and a short tail. Holding the tail end, twist your hand and the pliers to start bending the wire into a loop around the top jaw of the pliers. Using your free thumb, continue working the tail around the top jaw of the pliers until it is pointing the same way as the stem. Release your grip on the pliers but do not remove them. Rotate the pliers until you have one jaw above the loop. Now finish the loop by moving the tail all of the way around the plier jaw so that it crosses the stem.

★☆☆ **Skill level**   🕐 **1 hour**   **Techniques:** *Making a headpin loop p.14*

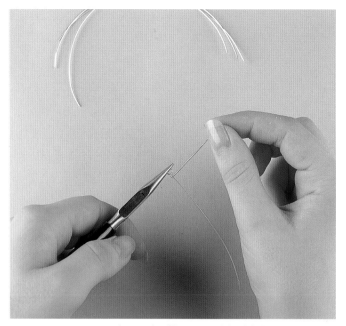

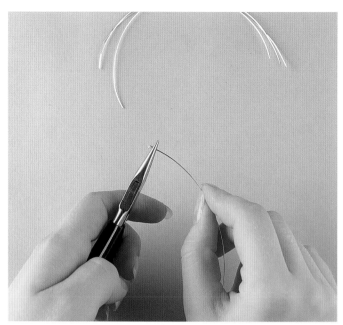

2 Do not cut the tail off. Instead hold the loop between the jaws of a pair of flat-nose pliers where the wire crosses itself. Keep the tail of the loop above the stem. Holding the end of the tail of wire, pull and wrap it under and around the stem two or three times.

3 Trim what is left of the tail as close to the stem as possible, and tuck in and crimp the remaining tail with the pliers. Squash the first coil, the one next to the loop, so that it grips the stem. Now use wire cutters to cut off the loop as close to the bottom coil as possible. This will stop the beads from falling off.

4 Thread on as many rose quartz tumbled chips as you like. Once you have the desired length, leave at least 2½ inches at the top to re-create the same coil effect as the bottom. Leave a small gap between the top tumbled chip and the start of the loop.

5 Follow Steps 1 and 2 to make the top loop and coil. Do not cut off the loop, because it will be used to connect the earring pin to the fishhook. Trim and crimp in the tail of the coil to neaten.

6 Make a second pin with mother-of-pearl tumbled chips, using a few more beads to make a slightly longer pin. With round-nose pliers, twist open the loop on a silver fishhook and thread each pin through it. Twist close the fishhook loop and repeat all the steps to make the second of the pair.

Helpful hint
For the best effect, vary the lengths of the pins when you have more than one pin on each fishhook.

Variation

Lace agate and amethyst earrings

These simple earrings can be made in a whole range of colors and lengths. This slightly longer pair uses blue lace agate, which is believed to promote healing, and amethyst, believed to promote intelligence.

Sunset crystal necklace

ROBIN BELLINGHAM

Most beading projects are designed as symmetrical patterns. Even when a random design is desired, the beader will generally fall into creating a pattern. The beads on this necklace may follow a roughly measured repetition, but the project features a random mix of colors and is a simple way of using up spare crystals and seed beads.

Don't be tempted to use cyanoacrylate glue, which is hard to control. If it gets on the beads, it gives them a frosty white coating.

You will need

Materials

- 4 lengths of clear monofilament: 15, 16, 17, and 18 inches
- 2 gold-plated necklace ends
- 2 crimps
- a selection of ⅙-inch crystal beads in oranges, reds, and golds (about 30)
- a selection of silver-lined seed beads, sizes 10 and 11, in topaz AB, orange AB, gold, orange, and red (about 80)

- Clear bead glue
- Gold-plated trigger clasp
- ¼-inch gold-plated jump ring

Tools

- Scissors
- Flat-nose pliers
- Small container

1 Thread all four strands of clear monofilament through a necklace end and then a crimp. At the end of the threads, crush the crimp bead against the threads with flat-nose pliers and trim away any excess. Close the necklace end over the crimp with the pliers.

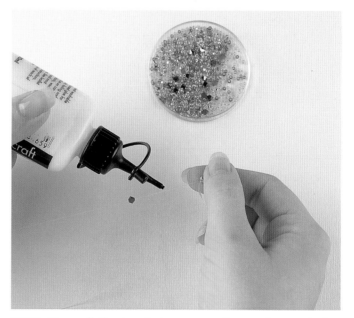

2 Pour all the beads into a small container to help you pick out the beads at random. Each bead is secured onto an individual thread with a very small amount of glue. Put a small dot of glue on the strand where you want the first bead to sit, then move the bead onto the glue.

★☆☆ **Skill level**   🕐 **3 hours**   **Techniques:** *Necklace ends p. 14*

3 Working on one thread at a time, continue adding more random beads. Space the beads approximately ½ to 1 inch apart. The spacing doesn't have to be exact because the scattered effect adds to the look and texture of the necklace.

Helpful hint

You may find it easier to control the amount of glue you use if you dispense it with a needle or headpin.

4 When each of the strands has been decorated with the desired number of beads, leave the glue to dry. Then thread all the strands through a necklace end and another crimp. Make sure the threads aren't twisted before you crush the crimp with pliers.

5 Close the necklace end over the crimp, hook the metal tail of the necklace end onto a gold-plated trigger clasp, and loop it back on itself to close. Attach a jump ring to the other necklace end in the same way.

Helpful hint
If you have enough time, it is easier to work if you leave each strand to dry before starting on the next.

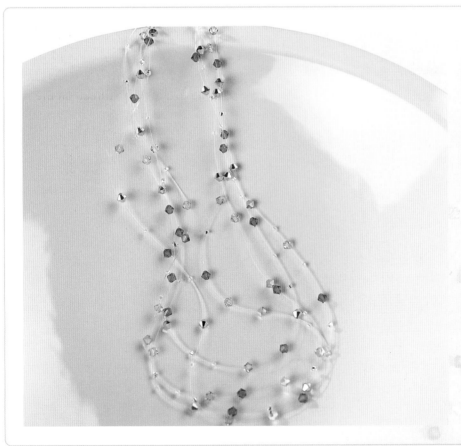

Variation

Silver and pink combination

This style of necklace will work in any color combination; just remember to alter the color of the clasp you use to suit the shade of the beads. Use gold-plated with warm colors and silver-plated with cool colors.

Beaded hair comb

JEMA HEWITT

Whether your hair is long or short, this beaded comb is sure to show it off to its full potential. The thick cluster of sparkle is just the thing to wear with a simple party dress. It is so easy to make, you could create one for every occasion. This project uses basic manipulation of wire and a variety of beads to create a very rich texture.

In pastel shades the comb would look wonderful as a bridesmaid's accessory.

You will need

Materials

- 80-inch length of 27-gauge silver-plated wire
- 18 ⅙-inch silver-colored pearl beads
- 3 ⅕-inch dark red crystal beads
- 18 ⅙-inch green fire polish beads
- Plain hair comb
- Assortment of size 10 seed beads and crystal beads up to ⅓ inch in various green colors

Tools

- Tape measure
- Wire cutters

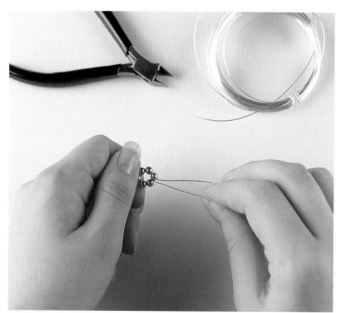

1 Start by making the flowers. Cut 6 inches of wire and thread on six ⅙-inch silver pearl beads. Push them halfway down the wire and twist the wire around until the beads form a circle. Twist the wire twice to hold the beads in place.

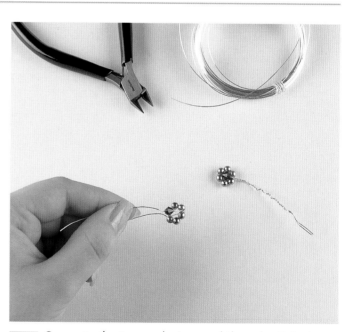

2 Separate the two end wires and thread a ⅕-inch dark red crystal bead on one strand. Push one wire to the front and one to the back of the pearl flower and position the crystal in the center. Twist the two wire strands together to hold the crystal in place. Make three flowers in the same way.

★☆☆ **Skill level**   🕐 **3 hours**

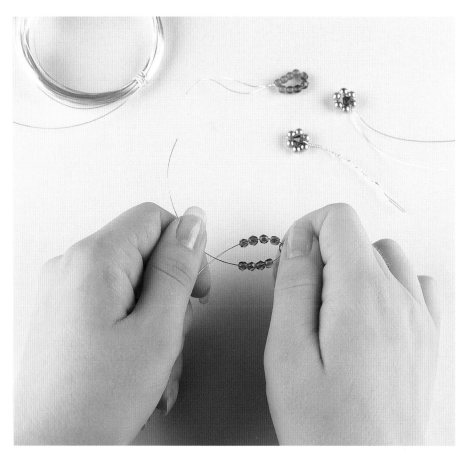

3 To make the leaves, thread nine ⅙-inch fire polish beads onto a 4-inch length of wire. Push them to the middle of the wire. Loop the wire around to make a leaf shape and twist the ends of the wire all the way down. Make two leaves. Twist together the wire stem of one leaf and one flower. Twist the second leaf and the remaining two flowers together. Bend the wires at a 45-degree angle, ³/8 inch from the heads. This is so that the flowers and leaves stand upright when you wrap them round the comb.

4 Cut 20 inches of wire and attach it to the comb at the left end by firmly wrapping it around three times. Hold one of the flower bunches along the length of the comb so the flower heads stand upright on the left. Wrap the long piece of wire around twice, very tightly, to begin securing.

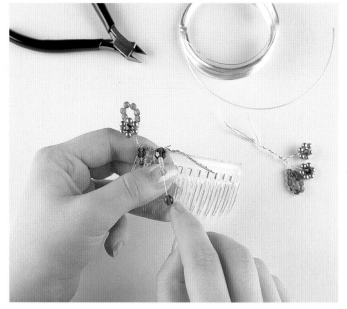

5 Thread a random selection of beads onto the end of the wire and start wrapping the beaded wire around the comb, working down from left to right. When you have covered about ³/4 inch add the next flower bunch. Continue wrapping the beaded wire, adding more beads as necessary.

6 Fasten by tightly wrapping unbeaded wire along the whole length of the comb three times. Trim the wire and tweak the flowers and leaves until they make a pleasing arrangement.

Helpful hint
For a vintage look, use a metal comb instead of an acrylic one. It will also last longer.

Variation

Red and gold alternative

These combs are a wonderful way to display individual special beads, so use the same techniques to make variations on the theme, experimenting with different colors.

Turquoise charm bracelet

JEMA HEWITT

This simple bracelet is a perfect way to display a selection of precious art beads, homemade beads, pendants, and charms. I fell in love with the turquoise rabbit and just had to show him off, so I chose greens and blues with lapis lazuli tumbled chips to complement it. This project is also a good way to use up leftover ⅓-inch beads. The more interesting the mix of bead types, the better the end effect.

Bracelets with personalized charms make wonderful presents.

You will need

Materials

- 6 charms, pendants, or art beads
- 6 sterling-silver jump rings or headpins
- A few assorted size 10 seed beads
- 2 sterling-silver necklace ends
- 6-inch length of 27-gauge tigertail
- 2 silver crimps
- Cyanoacrylate glue (optional)
- 14 ⅓-inch round beads, a mix of plain and faceted glass and crystal
- 13 large tumblechips
- Sterling-silver clasp

Tools

- 2 pairs of flat-nose pliers
- Round-nose pliers
- Wire cutters

1 First make the charms and beads ready to dangle. If a charm or pendant has a hole at the top, a jump ring can be attached and closed. Choose a jump ring that is big enough to leave a gap at the top for the bracelet cord. Twist the ring with two pairs of pliers to open, insert through the pendant hole and twist back again to close.

Helpful hint
If you have a brittle crystal charm, use a triangular clamp instead.

★☆☆ **Skill level**   🕐 **3 hours**   **Techniques:** *Opening and closing jump rings, Making headpin loops, Necklace ends p. 14*

2 If the hole goes from the top to the bottom of the bead, place it on a headpin with a seed bead or two at the top and bottom, so the charm doesn't fall off. Make a loop at the top of the headpin with round-nose pliers. To do this, curve the wire around the pliers leaving a tail. Grip the loop flat in flat-nose pliers and wrap the wire around the stem a few times to finish. Trim any spare wire with wire cutters.

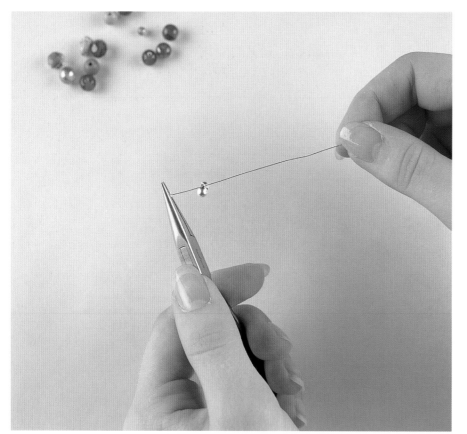

3 Cut a 6-inch length of tigertail, and thread on a necklace end and then a crimp. Push to the end of the tigertail and crush the crimp with the flat-nose pliers. Make sure it is completely secure; then close up the necklace end very gently over the crimp with the pliers. For extra security you could put a dab of glue on the crimp too.

Helpful hint
Tigertail is very strong but you could use beading thread instead.

4 Place the ⅓-inch round beads and tumbled chips in front of you in a pleasing but random arrangement. Thread on a bead, a tumbled chip, another bead, a tumbled chip, and a charm. Repeat the pattern until you have used all the beads and charms.

5 Attach the final necklace end as before and trim any excess tigertail with wire cutters. Add a silver clasp, attaching each end to the necklace ends by closing the loops with round-nose pliers.

Variation

Charm ideas

Always keep an eye out for special beads to use as charms, or try making your own from polymer clay.

Victorian drop necklace

HANA GLOVER

This elegant project was inspired by the beautiful Victorian jet necklaces and collars that became popular after Queen Victoria went into mourning following the death of her beloved husband, Albert. Although I have chosen pretty, light colors for this project, almost any color combination would be effective.

A jet necklace, such as the variation on page 41, would traditionally be made from the famous Whitby jet.

You will need

Materials

- 6 ½-foot length of 23-gauge lilac beading thread
- 2 silver necklace ends
- ½ ounce of size 7 crystal AB seed beads
- 12 ⅙-inch violet bicone beads
- 8 ¼-inch violet bicone drop beads
- Cyanoacrylate glue (optional)
- Triangular clamp
- Large crystal AB drop pendant
- Necklace tag
- Trigger clasp

Tools

- Scissors
- Flexible beading needle (optional)
- Flat-nose pliers

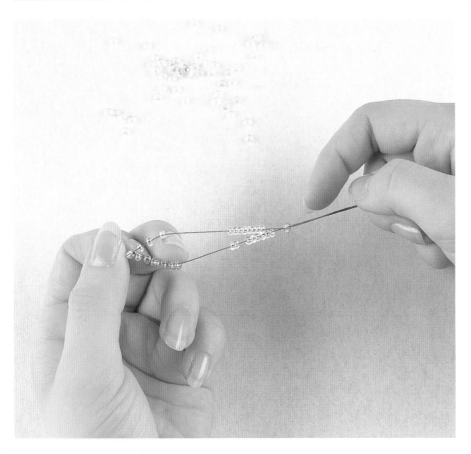

1 Cut two 30-inch lengths of beading thread. Push both ends through a necklace end, knot together, and close the necklace end over the knot with flat-nose pliers. Thread 11 size 7 seed beads onto one thread and 15 onto the other thread. Add a ⅙-inch bicone bead, threading it through both threads, and pull tight. The lower thread will now form a loop underneath the first one.

2 Thread 20 size 7 seed beads onto the lower thread. On the top thread, add six size 7 seed beads, one ¼-inch bicone drop bead then another six size 7 seed beads. Then thread a ⅙-inch bicone onto both threads. This forms the second loop.

Helpful hint
If you find it difficult to thread the beads, use a flexible beading needle or apply cyanoacrylate glue to the ends of the thread to stiffen them.

3 Add 25 size 7 seed beads onto the lower thread. Thread eight size 7 seeds, one ¼-inch bicone drop, and eight size 7 seeds onto the top thread; then pass both threads through a ⅙-inch bicone bead. Thread 30 size 7 seeds onto the lower thread. Onto the top thread add 10 size 7 seeds, one ¼-inch bicone and 10 size 7 seeds; then thread both ends through a ⅙-inch bicone. To the lower thread add 15 size 7 seeds, a ⅙-inch bicone and 15 size 7 seeds. On the top thread add 12 size 7 seeds, one ¼-inch bicone drop, and 12 size 7 seeds. Then thread both ends through a ⅙-inch bicone bead.

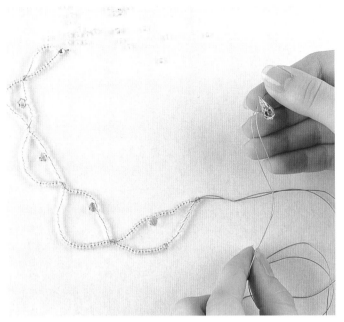

4 Attach a triangular clamp to a large crystal AB drop pendant. Thread both threads through the clamp. Add another $\frac{1}{6}$-inch bicone bead, then continue making loops mirroring the other side of the necklace (following the instructions in the opposite direction to make loops that decrease in size).

5 When all of the loops have been made, add a necklace end with flat-nose pliers. Hook the metal tail of the neckace end through a necklace tag, and close the loop with flat-nose pliers. Attach a trigger clasp to the other necklace end in the same way.

Variation

Traditional drop necklace

This version shows how Victorian traditional necklaces looked. It makes a very elegant evening accessory for formal events.

Candy-stripe bead choker

ROBIN BELLINGHAM

Peyote stitch is one of many bead weaving stitches, and an easy type to master. When using Delica beads, leave no gaps between the beads. Each bead should fit snugly with its neighbor, for a very tidy project. In this project, I have used even-count peyote stitch. You can see the pattern grow very quickly.

A small tube of peyote stitch bead weaving looks modern and dramatic on a plain necklace choker.

You will need

Materials

- 3-foot length of purple size D nylon thread or waxed thread
- ⅕ ounce of DB610 silver-lined violet size 11 Delicas (dark Delica bead)
- ⅕ ounce of DB041 silver-lined crystal size 11 Delicas (light Delica bead)
- Necklace choker with screw-off bead or similar necklace thread

Tools

- Masking tape
- Size 10 beading needle

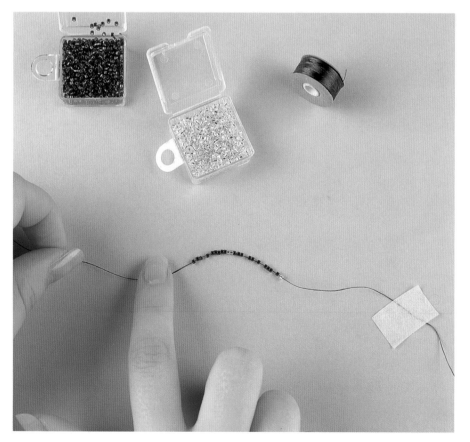

1 Start by taping the size D nylon thread or waxed thread to your work surface, about 4 inches from one end. Thread the beads from the other end, with the first bead stopping about about 4 inches from the tape. Thread on 22 beads in this order: 1 light, 10 dark, 2 light, 9 dark. Thread a beading needle onto the end of the thread.

Helpful hint
Use beeswax or a commercial thread conditioner on the thread to stop it from tangling.

★★☆ Skill level   🕐 2 hours   **Techniques:** *Peyote stitch p. 16*

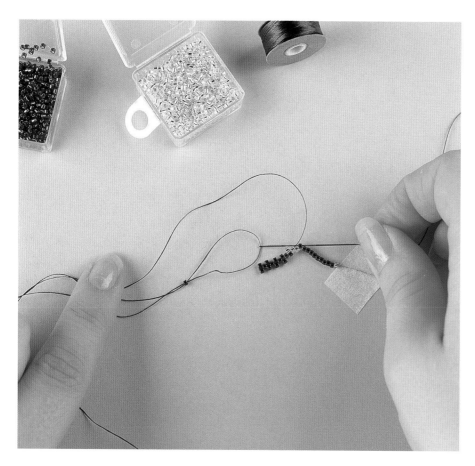

2 Add one dark bead (bead 23), then thread the needle through bead 21, skipping bead 22 and working toward the tape. Pull the thread through until beads 22 and 23 are side by side. Add a second dark bead, skip one bead, and thread through bead 19. Pull the thread; bead 19 will push bead 20 and the dark bead side by side. A pattern will start developing. Each time you add a bead, skip the next bead on the original 22 beads and thread through the next one in line. You will only be threading through the odd-numbered beads. The fifth bead, added when threading back toward the tape, should be a light color. Add four more dark beads as above; the last bead on this row should be a light color.

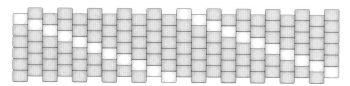

3 You will notice a pattern of beads that stick out from the main body of beads. Thread through each of these beads after you have added each of the following beads in succession. **Row 4:** (working away from the tape) add 1 dark (thread through); add 1 light (thread through); add 1 dark (thread through); add 1 dark (thread through); add 1 dark (thread through); add 1 dark (thread through); add 1 dark (thread through); add 1 light (thread through); add 1 dark (thread through); add 1 dark (thread through); add 1 dark (thread through). **Row 5:** (working toward the tape) 3 dark; 1 light; 5 dark; 1 light; 1 dark. **Row 6:** (working away from the tape) 2 dark; 1 light; 5 dark; 1 light; 2 dark. **Row 7:** (working toward the tape) 2 dark; 1 light; 5 dark; 1 light; 2 dark. **Row 8:** (working away from the tape) 3 dark; 1 light; 5 dark; 1 light; 1 dark. **Row 9:** (working toward the tape) 1 dark; 1 light; 5 dark; 1 light; 3 dark. **Row 10:** (working away from the tape) 4 dark; 1 light; 5 dark; 1 light. **Row 11:** (working toward the tape) 1 light; 4 dark; 1 light; 5 dark. **Row 12:** (working away from the tape) 5 dark; 1 light; 5 dark.

4 Once you have completed these 12 rows, you should be in the position to sew the two long edges together. If you bring both edges together you will find that they sit snugly. Sew through each edge bead, sewing from one bead through the next bead until you have a complete tube. Hide the tail of thread by weaving back through the pattern until you lose the tail or you are satisfied that you can cut it. Repeat for the other tail, at the beginning of the peyote stitch.

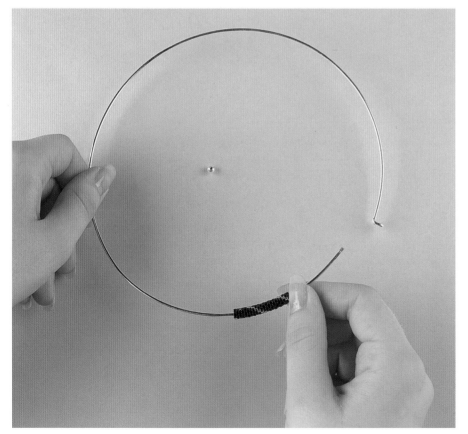

5 Unscrew the bead tip from the necklace choker and thread on the peyote-stitch tube. Gently push it around to the front of the choker and replace the bead tip.

Helpful hint
You could also continue the peyote-stitch pattern to make a longer length tube.

Embroidered bag

JEMA HEWITT

Once you have learned the techniques for sewing beads onto fabric you just won't be able to stop. In Elizabethan times, clothes were embroidered with real pearls and precious gems. In the 1920s beads were used all over fine fabrics to add weight and texture. Today, richly beaded clothing has enjoyed a renewed popularity.

This gorgeous beaded purse uses a variety of techniques as inspiration and the design can be placed on any surface, such as the edge of a shawl or as decoration on a blouse or bodice.

You will need

Materials

- A ready-made purse or bag
- Tailor's chalk pencil, in a shade close to the bag color, or tailor's carbon paper and wheel
- Sewing thread
- Approximately 40 size 10 seed beads
- Approximately 15 ⅙-inch crystal beads
- Approximately 80 bugle beads

Tools

- Size 10 beading needle

1 Make sure the bag you have chosen is not made with tightly stretched material or it will be very difficult to embroider. The best type is a gathered pouch.

2 Photocopy the template on page 78, enlarging if necessary. Draw the design freehand with a chalk pencil, using the photocopy as a guide. Or, use tailor's carbon paper and wheel to trace the main elements of the design. You do not need to transfer every single bead placement, just the main parts so the finished piece will be in proportion.

★★☆ **Skill level**   🕐 **3 hours**   **Techniques:** *Beaded backstitch p. 15*

3 Thread the needle and tie a knot in the end of the thread. Bring the needle up through the fabric, starting in the center of the design, and sew on a central seed bead and the five crystals using a beaded backstitch. (See page 15.) Next, attach the bugle beads one by one in a swirl on either side of the cluster. Be careful not to catch the lining when sewing. If you have to move the thread across a large distance under the work, don't pull it too tight. Take a little stitch to hold it before starting the next row of beads. You may find it easier to place the bag on your hand when sewing, rather than on the table.

4 Sew on all the other bugle beads in the same way. Next, attach the crystal beads firmly. Stitch through each one a couple of times because heavy beads will wear the thread quickly.

Helpful hint
If you are embroidering a home-sewn item, do the beadwork embellishment before assembling the piece.

5 Finally, attach the seed beads into place using a beaded backstitch. (See page 15.) If you need to add thread, finish by stitching over and over in an inconspicuous place and snip the tail close to the fabric. Start new thread by stitching over and over under the first bead to be sewn on. Don't be afraid to unpick and start again if a bead isn't quite where you want it. Also be patient and try to judge the overall effect before deciding whether the bead is really noticeably wrong.

Variation

Your own design

Designing your own embroidery is very rewarding. Take inspiration from patterns and motifs on wallpaper, fabric, and even ceramic items. Each era in history has its own distinct style, and books on historical decoration are invaluable. Think about the type of bead to use. Dense areas of seed beads, for example, can have a great effect, as can sequins.

Bead-loom bracelet

HANA GLOVER

Native American beadwork was traditionally made with materials such as shell, bone, and turquoise. When the Americas were colonized, European beads, such as glass pony beads and seed beads, were introduced. They were originally available only in a small number of opaque colors.

This design is inspired by the traditional colors and the geometric patterns favored by some tribes. I have used a toggle clasp to fasten the bracelet because it is much easier to manage with one hand.

You will need

Materials

- Strong sewing thread, in a color to match the beads
- Size 10 seed beads in opaque blue, opaque red, opaque light blue, and opaque turquoise (approximately 120 of each color)
- Glue
- 2 necklace ends
- Toggle clasp

Tools

- Tape measure
- Bead loom
- Flat-nose pliers
- Size 10 beading needle
- Flexible beading needle

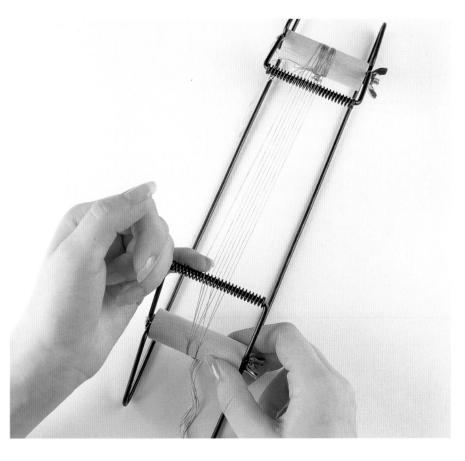

1 Measure out eight 20-inch lengths of thread. Knot them together at one end. Hook the knot over the nail (anchor) at one end of a bead loom. Wrap the thread around the spool and tighten the nut. Separate the threads on the spring so that each one is in a separate groove, next to the previous one. Tie the other end of the thread and repeat the process on the other end of the loom. Make sure the threads do not cross over each other and that they are taut. These are the warp threads.

2   Thread another 5 feet of thread onto a beading needle. Knot the thread onto the warp thread furthest left at the bottom of the loom, next to the spring. Leave a 4-inch tail. This is the weft thread. Thread seven blue seed beads onto the needle. Place the needle underneath the warp threads, push the beads up so that one bead sits between each of the warp threads. Then pull the needle and thread through the beads, using your finger to hold the beads in position. To secure the beads in place, bring the needle to the front of the loom and thread it back through the beads in the opposite direction. Pull the thread tight and straighten out the line.

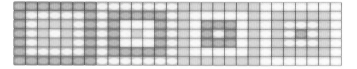

4   Continue adding the beads row by row, following the pattern above, until the bracelet is the desired length. To make a necklace, book mark, or belt, follow the above instructions, but alter the length of the warp threads. They should be the length of the desired finished item plus 16 inches.

3   Thread one blue, five turquoise, and then one more blue bead. Hold the needle underneath the warp threads with the beads spaced one between each thread. As before, pull the needle and thread through the beads underneath the warp threads, then back through them in the opposite direction on top of the warp threads. Pull tight and straighten the beads.

5 To make the item longer than the loom, loosen the nuts and gently lift the work off the springs. Move it down the loom to where there is enough space to continue. Tighten the nuts, and bead as before.

6 When the bracelet is complete, loosen the nuts and remove it from the loom. Knot the warp threads in adjacent pairs, with the exception of the last knot, which will also include the weft thread. Repeat at the other end of the bracelet.

7 Thread the two knotted threads on the left onto a flexible beading needle. Thread through the first three seed beads, from the left, toward the center of the bracelet. Repeat with the threads on the right so that all the threads are in the center. Now use the flexible beading needle to thread all of the strands through a necklace end. Knot the threads together and put a dot of glue on the knot. Then close a necklace end over it with flat-nose pliers. Hook on one end of a toggle clasp and close the loop of the necklace end by squeezing gently with a pair of flat-nose pliers. Repeat on the other end of the bracelet.

Beaded pillow tassel

JEMA HEWITT

I adore tassels. There is something about them that transforms the most mundane item into one that is really sophisticated. The flappers of the 1920s knew this and used tassels on coats, dresses, handbags—and even necklaces. This pillow cover is elevated to a wonderful chic accessory that any sofa would be proud to wear.

If pillows aren't your thing, why not add a tassel to a light pull, a purse, or the end of your sewing scissors?

You will need

Materials

- Very fine, silky thread, machine embroidery cotton is good
- 4 x 6-inch rectangle of cardboard
- Strong buttonhole thread, in the same color as the embroidery thread
- ½ ounce of size 10 seed beads in two contrasting colors
- 3-foot length of gold size D nylon thread or waxed thread

- Ready-made pillow cover
- Glue (optional)

Tools

- Tape measure
- Scissors
- Size 10 beading needle
- Sewing needle

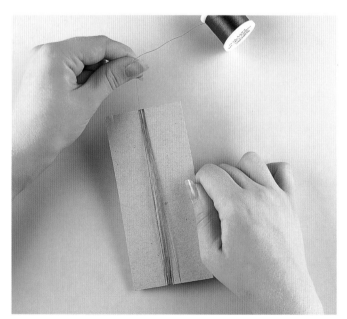

1 To make the basic tassel, wrap fine embroidery thread around the longest part of a cardboard rectangle. About 200 wraps of the finest thread is enough; use less if it's a thicker cotton. If you want more than one tassel, count how many wraps you have made so that each tassel has the same plumpness.

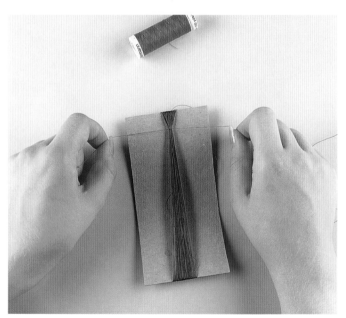

2 Cut 8 inches of buttonhole thread, and tuck it between the threads and cardboard. Pull the buttonhole thread to the top edge of the cardboard, and tie a square or reef knot very tightly to bind the embroidery threads together. Don't trim the long buttonhole threads yet.

 Skill level ☆☆☆   🕐 **3 hours**   **Techniques:** *Peyote stitch p. 16*

3 Holding the top part of the tassel in one hand, snip the bottom loops of the threads at the edge of the cardboard. Cut a length of the fine embroidery thread and wrap it tightly around the top ½ inch of the tassel, creating a wrapped head. Tie the ends in a square or reef knot and trim. Trim the bottom edge evenly, as well.

Helpful hint
Use small, very sharp scissors to trim the tassel.

4 Make a square of peyote stitch by attaching a stopper bead to about 3 feet of size D nylon thread or waxed thread. Loop the thread and needle back through a seed bead to stop it from moving. Thread 12 alternately colored seed beads. Work peyote stitches by picking up a bead of the same color as the last one, and pass the needle back down through the opposite-color bead that is next to it. Work your way down the row, adding a bead of one color, but passing the needle through the beads of the opposite color. (See page 16.)

5 Keep the tension firm and, when you have about eight beads at the top and bottom of the piece, check the size by wrapping it around the tassel head. It should fit tightly. If it is too small, add more rows until it fits comfortably. Make sure the beads sticking out on each side are opposite colors. Sew together the two long edges, threading the needle through one bead on each side. Finish the thread off by weaving through the beads.

6 Slip the beaded head over the silk tassel, if you want to make it very firm, either glue it into place or sew through it a few times.

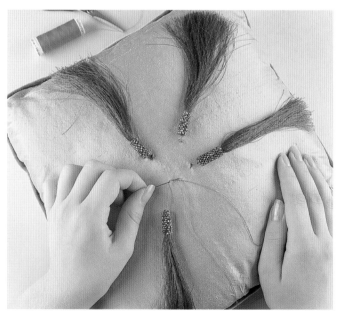

7 Attach the tassel to the cushion cover using the two long buttonhole threads and a sharp sewing needle. Just sew over and over, very neatly, and trim the excess thread. Sew the tassels fairly close to the cushion but not so tight that they don't lie properly.

Flower choker card

HANA GLOVER

Handmade cards are wonderful presents with a personal touch. Combining them with an item of jewelry is a perfect gift that will be treasured. This design is inspired by French-beaded flowers, which are thought to date back to the fifteenth century.

French-beaded flowers can be very beautiful, but they are time-consuming and complicated to make. This design is a quicker and flatter piece that is ideal for mounting on ribbon or cardstock.

You will need

Materials

- 3-foot length of 30-gauge clear monofilament
- 12 size 7 seed beads
- ½ ounce size 10 transparent blue seed beads
- ½ ounce size 10 silver-lined blue seed beads
- 1 ½-inch faceted blue bead
- 20-inch length of wired fabric ribbon (reasonably sturdy to hold weight of flower)
- Glue
- Iron-on plastic hook-and-loop tape

- Sewing thread
- Coordinating card and envelope
- Double-sided tape (optional)

Tools

- Tape measure
- Scissors
- Iron
- Sewing needle

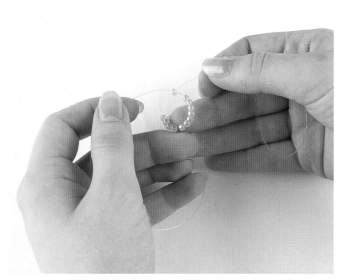

1 To make the flower, thread 12 size 7 seed beads onto the monofilament. Pass the thread through all seven beads again in the same direction and through the first bead for a third time. Pull tight to form a circle, leaving an 8-inch tail. You will need this in Step 6.

2 Thread 16 size 10 transparent blue seed beads onto the longer end of the monofilament. Thread around the outside of the end bead, then back through the next bead toward the circle. This forms the tip of the petal.

★★☆ **Skill level** 🕐 **3 hours**

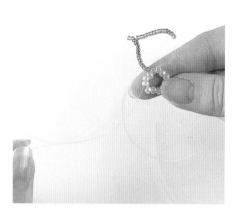

3 Thread 14 transparent blue seed beads. Starting two beads away from where the petal begins, thread back through (against the direction of the thread) five beads of the circle. Pull tight. This is the first petal.

4 Thread 16 transparent blue seed beads. Take the thread around the end bead, and then thread it back through the next bead. Add 14 more seed beads, and, starting at the size 7 bead, two beads back from where the petal started, thread back through the last five beads. Repeat the steps until four petals have been made.

5 To make the inner petals, thread through the next size 7 bead in the circle. Thread on 14 size 10 silver-lined blue seed beads, take the thread around the end bead, and then thread it back through the next one. Add 12 seed beads then thread back through the last size 7 bead. Thread through the next three seed beads in the circle.

6 Repeat Step 5 until four inner petals have been made. To add the center of the flower, thread on an 1/3-inch faceted blue bead, then thread through the size 7 bead on the opposite side of the circle. Pass the thread back through the size 7 beads of the circle until it is next to the tail thread. Tie the two threads together using a reef knot. The flower is now complete.

Helpful hint
This project should be made with monofilament, which adds shape to the petals while going through the beads several times.

7 Neatly trim one end of a 20-inch length of ribbon and dip it in glue to prevent fraying. Leave it to dry. Measure the ribbon to the exact length for a choker, approximately 14 inches. This may vary from person to person so, if possible, check in advance. Leave an extra 2 inches then cut and treat the end with glue. Cut 1½ inches of iron-on hook-and-loop tape, and following the manufacturer's instructions, press one side of the tape onto each end of the ribbon. Sew the flower onto the center of the ribbon.

8 Wrap the ribbon around the card, using the hook-and-loop tape to fasten it on the inside of the card. The wire in the ribbon should hold it in place. If not, a strip of double-sided tape will secure it.

Helpful hint
If you can't find any monofilament, it is available at fishing tackle shops.

Spiral-rope bracelet

JEMA HEWITT

Spiral rope is one of the easiest but most rewarding bead-weaving stitches. As an added bonus it grows really quickly. This three-strand bracelet uses exquisite Japanese bugle beads to create a helter-skelter type design. You could also use contrasting colors or different-sized seed beads instead of bugles for an alternative.

This project would be equally effective as a choker. Use Japanese bugles, however, because Czech bugles have sharp edges that will tear through the thread very quickly.

You will need

Materials

- 10-foot turquoise size D nylon thread or waxed thread
- 1/3 ounce of size 9 seed beads
- 6 sterling-silver necklace ends
- 1/2 ounce of Japanese bugle beads
- 4 3-strand spacer bars
- Three-strand sterling-silver clasp

Tools

- Scissors
- Size 10 beading needle
- Flat-nose pliers

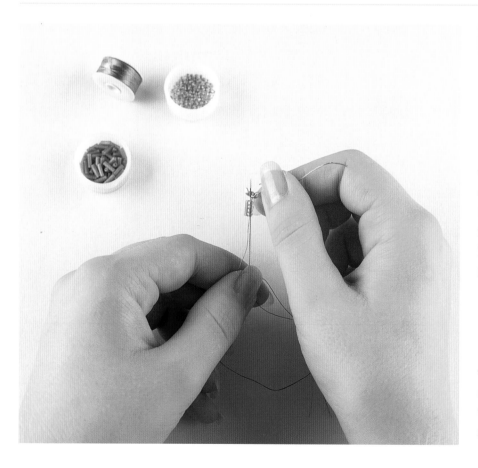

1 Cut 20 inches of size D nylon thread or waxed thread and, using a beading needle, thread on one seed bead. Go through the bead again and tie a reef knot to secure it. Thread on a necklace end, positioned so the seed bead will be contained in it when shut. Thread on four seed beads and a bugle bead. Pass the needle up through the necklace end, through the seed bead, then back down through the necklace end and four seed beads.

Helpful hint

If you need to undo some work, unthread the needle and pull the thread through from the bead end, not back up through the work.

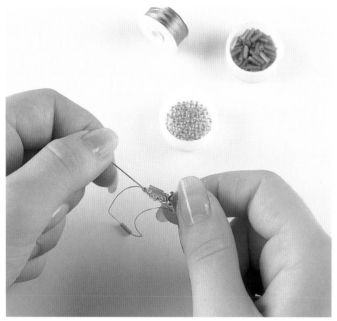

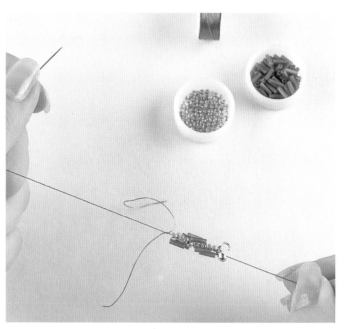

2 To start the spiral, add one seed bead and one bugle bead. Push them down to the others. Pass the needle up through the top four seed beads, leaving out the bottom seed (the one next to the necklace end). Arrange the second bugle so it lies to the right of the first bugle. You will see the beads begin to step up.

3 Continue adding a seed and bugle and passing the needle through the previous four seeds. Make sure each new bugle lies to the right of the one before or it won't spiral properly. If you need to add thread, leave a long end and tie a reef knot. Weave the two ends into the spiral very securely.

4 Repeat until you have added 18 bugles. Now thread a spacer bar, four seeds, and a bugle. Pass the needle back down through the spacer bar, through the last bugle and last four seeds. Then go back up through the spacer bar and the top four seeds. Add a seed and a bugle and continue making the spiral as before. Repeat for another 18 bugles and add a spacer bar in the same way until you have three space bars and four sets of spirals.

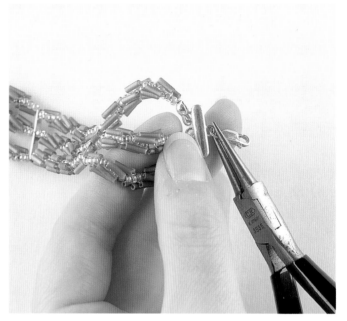

5 Finish with 18 more bugles. Then thread a necklace end followed by a seed bead. Loop back through the seed bead, down through the necklace end, through the top four seeds, up through the bugle and the necklace end, and through the seed bead. Repeat this sequence a few times until it's secure.

6 Create two more strands in the same way. Pass the second strand through the center holes of the spacer bar and the final strand through the bottom holes. Close the necklace ends very gently over the seed bead. Finally attach the necklace ends to the clasp with flat-nose pliers.

Variation

Other ideas

This choker is made from three rows of spiral rope with two lengths of beads in between. A single strand made from two sizes of seed bead makes a simple accessory.

Knotted pearl necklace

ROBIN BELLINGHAM

This three-strand knotted pearl necklace is a timeless classic. It has a simple elegance and doesn't necessarily need an occasion to be worn. Pearls have always been spaced with knots to prevent them from chipping. Another reason for knotting is so that you won't lose many pearls if the necklace breaks.

Gimp or French wire is a finely spun coil of wire, which is used on the exposed thread at the clasp. Its primary purpose is to protect the thread from wear and tear so that the necklace lasts longer.

You will need

Materials

- 76 ⅙-inch pearls (pre-strung)
- 68 ⅕-inch pearls (pre-strung)
- 60 ¼-inch pearls (pre-strung)
- Headpin or stiff beading needle
- Gimp (French wire)
- Multi-strand or 3-strand clasp
- Glue

Tools

- Flexible beading needle
- Scissors

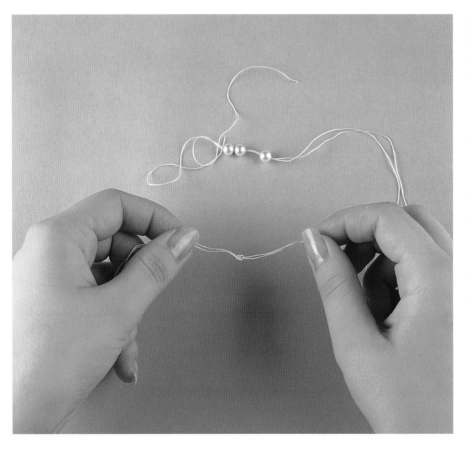

1 The three strands uses pearls of different sizes. Always tackle the smallest pearl strand first. This will set the length of the multi-strand necklace. The other two strands should hang lower each time in order to give the required effect. Pre-strung pearls are the most handy beads to use for this project. Tie a knot at each end of the strand. Separate the first three pearls from the majority and push to the end. You will need these at the end of the project when you come to attach the clasp. Leave a 12-inch gap and then tie another knot.

Helpful hint
For a quicker project, make a single-stranded necklace.

★★★ **Skill level**   🕐 **7 hours**

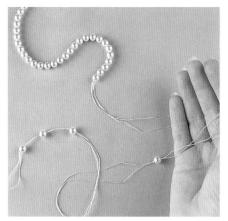

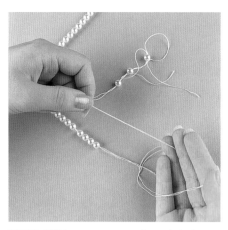

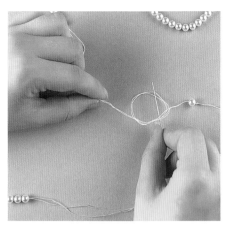

2 Move one pearl from the majority up against the first knot you have tied. Now hold one hand flat and drape the pearls over your hand so that the three separated pearls are in front of your fingers and the majority of the pearls are hanging behind. The front pearls should hang below your hand. You should have a front thread and a back thread.

3 With your spare hand, bring the front thread around behind the back thread and up and over to the front of the second and third finger. Grip the thread with these two fingers.

4 Pull this thread so that your hand is pulling out of the loop you have just made. With one finger, pull this loose knot close to the pearl with which you are working. Place a beading needle or headpin in the center of the knot so that it doesn't tie itself together.

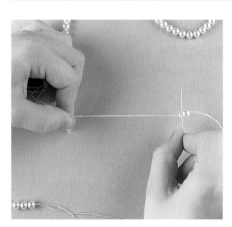

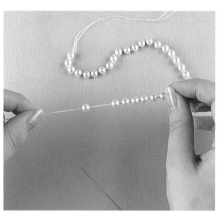

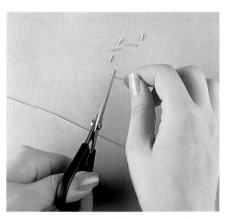

5 Use the needle to move the knot up against the pearl being held by the first knot. Once you have the knot as close to the pearl as possible, remove the needle and tighten the knot against the pearl.

6 Move another pearl from the majority up against the knot you have just tied and repeat from Step 3. Remember to regularly check the length of the strand you are knotting. Three pearls have to be left untied at each end to secure the clasp. Repeat this knotting procedure for the other two strands of pearls.

7 Cut six ½-inch pieces of gimp wire.

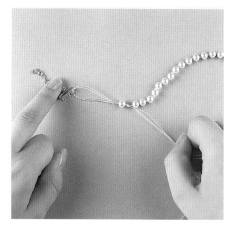

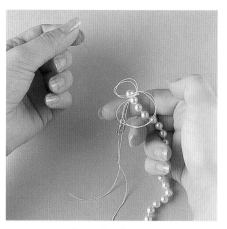

8 Holding the three loose pearls at one end of the strand cut off the knot. Push these three pearls against the rest of the knotted strand. Using a flexible beading needle, take the thread through one of the short lengths of gimp, then through one of the corresponding loops in a multi-strand clasp, and finally through the first of the three pearls.

9 Pull the thread until the gimp is looped through the clasp loop and there is no gap in the thread between the gimp and pearl. Allow a very small gap between the three pearls for a knot.

10 Tie a knot by forming a loop around the necklace strand with the loose end and tucking it up inside this loop.

11 Pull tight and use your needle to thread through the next bead. Tie a knot. Thread through the third bead, but this time, do not tie a knot. Just cut the thread as close to the pearl as possible. Add a dab of glue to each of the two knots you have just tied.

12 Make the other two strands in the same way. Test the length by closing the clasp and holding the second strand's loose end through the corresponding clasp loop. If you need to add one or more beads, repeat Steps 3–5 with the required number of beads. As long as you have one glued knot holding each end, it will suffice. Repeat Steps 8–11 until all three strands are complete.

Figure-eight earrings

ROBIN BELLINGHAM

This is the most challenging of my projects. I have made more earrings than I care to mention, using both mass-produced and handmade components. I prefer to make earrings from handmade components, which create totally unique pieces that can definitely be called "designer."

It will take some practise, but the end result will justify the means.

You will need

Materials

• 2 6-inch lengths of 20-gauge wire
• 2 8-inch lengths of 26-gauge silver-plated wire
• 4 4-inch lengths of 26-gauge wire
• 4 ⅙-inch lapis lazuli semiprecious beads
• 2 sterling-silver fishhooks

Tools

• Pen
• Wire cutters
• Flat-nose pliers
• Round-nose pliers

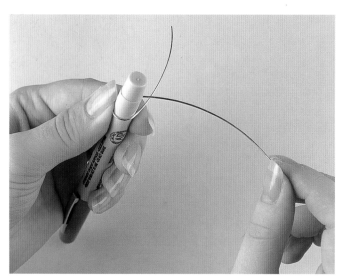

1 Mark 26-gauge wire on either side ½ inch from the center. Also mark the side of a pen. To make the first loop, align the mark on on end of the wire with the mark on the pen and curl the wire up and around, as shown.

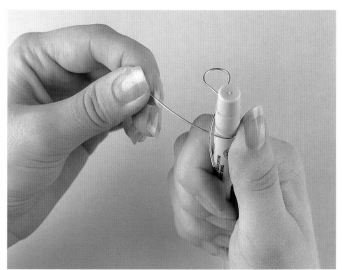

2 For the second loop, line up the mark on the other end of the wire with the mark on the pen. Working in the opposite direction, curl the wire down and around.

★★★ **Skill level**   🕐 **2 hours**   **Techniques:** *Making a headpin loop p. 14*

3 To make the center, use one 8-inch and one 4-inch length of 26-gauge wire. Approximately one third of the way down the longer piece, hold the shorter piece of wire against the longer one, leaving a ½-inch tail on the shorter wire. Pull the tail tightly around the long wire three or four times to form a coil. Add a semiprecious bead to the longer wire and hold it next to the coil you have just made. Wrap the shorter wire once around the bead then form a coil in the same fashion on the other side of the bead to secure it. Repeat this a second time to add another bead about one-third of the way down from the top of the opposite end of the same long piece of wire.

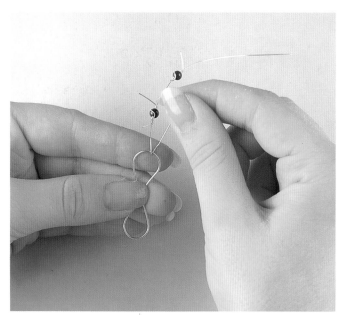

4 To attach the two pieces, adjust the beads and coils to sit in the center of each loop. Leave about 2 inches at the bottom of the shorter piece of wire to wrap around the bottom loop. Wrap around the eight shape twice each side of the center wire. Trim and tuck the end away with flat-nose pliers.

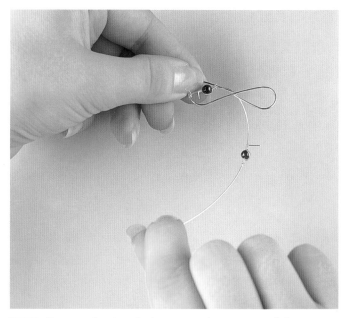

5 Secure the beaded wire to the center of the figure eight by wrapping it around three times. The first time you wrap it around the center you will need to hold it in place. Once it's in place, you can wrap it around a second time and then a third time without holding it.

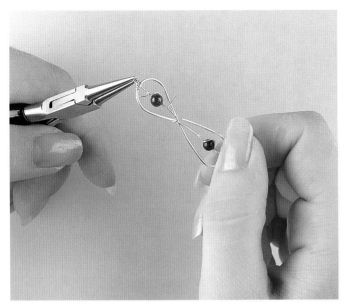

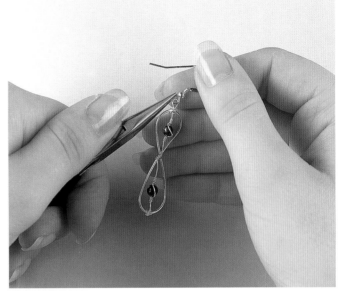

6 Wrap the wire over the top of the top loop, thread under, and wrap twice more. To make a loop at the top for hanging, wrap the wire around one side of a pair of round-nose pliers. Hold the pliers against the top of the figure eight. Wrap once around the plier jaw and figure eight, then twice more around the figure eight.

7 Trim and tuck the ends of each coil. Twist open the loop at the bottom of a fishhook, and hang the figure-eight earring from the open loop. Close the loop with pliers. Repeat for the second earring.

Variation

Variety of beads

These earrings work well with many beads, so why not try them with crystal beads for some extra sparkle? When you have mastered this project, you will want to make more.

Star choker necklace

HANA GLOVER

Stars and beads are two of my favorite things. This choker combines both of them. Once you've made your first star, you'll see how surprisingly easy it is to do.

Why not try other colors, or make a matching belt with larger beads?

You will need

Materials

- 5-foot length of green size D nylon thread or waxed thread
- Thread conditioner or beeswax
- Approximately 160 size 10/11 clear AB Delicas or seed beads
- Approximately 160 size 10/11 teal Delicas or seed beads
- Approximately 160 ⅓-inch bugle beads
- Trigger clasp and tag

Tools

- Size 10 beading needle

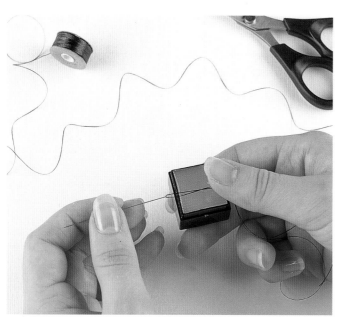

1 Thread a beading needle with 5 feet of size D nylon thread or waxed thread. Run the thread through thread conditioner or beeswax to coat the whole length. (This keeps the thread from knotting and fraying.) Run the thread through your fingers to remove any excess conditioner.

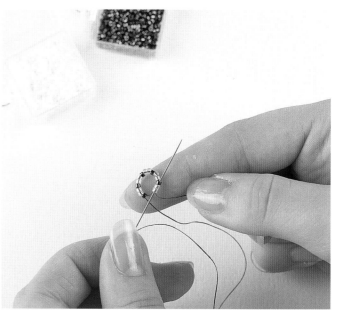

2 Thread on two AB beads and one teal bead. Repeat until you have 10 AB and five teal beads in a sequence. Push the beads to the end of the thread, leaving an 8-inch tail. Thread through these 15 beads again to form a circle. Thread through the next two AB beads and one teal bead to secure.

★★★ **Skill level**   🕑 **4 hours**

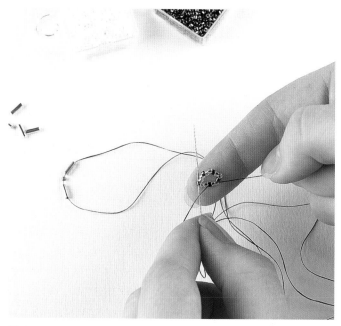

3 Add one bugle, one teal bead, and one bugle. Thread through the next teal bead in the circle.

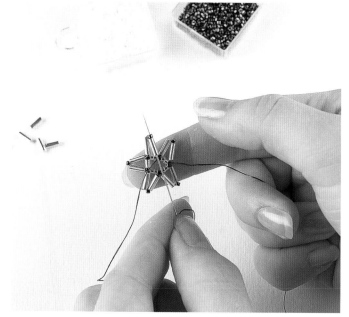

4 Add one bugle, one teal, and one bugle. Thread through the next teal bead in the circle. Repeat the process until all five points are complete. Thread through the adjacent bugle bead toward the point of the star and through the teal bead on the point.

5 Add one teal and one bugle to form the point of the next star. Thread on one teal and two AB beads, repeating until there are 15 beads in the sequence. Form a circle by threading through 13 beads again, missing two AB beads.

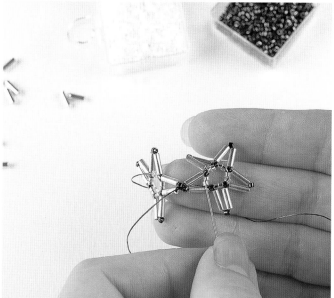

6 Add one bugle then thread through the teal bead to form the first point. Thread down toward the circle through one bugle then the next teal bead. Continue adding points until the star is complete. Thread through the circle to the point where you wish to add the next star.

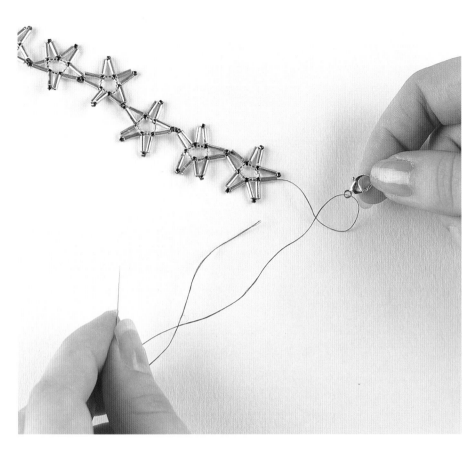

7 Continue adding stars until the necklace is the desired length. To add the trigger clasp, thread the needle through to the end of the point of the star where you want to attach the clasp. Thread on the clasp then back through the teal bead of the point to form a circle of thread. Repeat twice to strengthen the join. Thread down the nearest bugle; then knot around the thread. Thread through two AB beads; then knot around the thread. Thread through the next teal bead; then knot around the thread. Weave the thread through a few extra beads then cut.

8 Repeat the process at the other end of the necklace to attach the other side of the clasp.

Helpful hint
This necklace can also be made with all seed or Delica beads. The points are formed by missing the last bead and threading back through the next one.

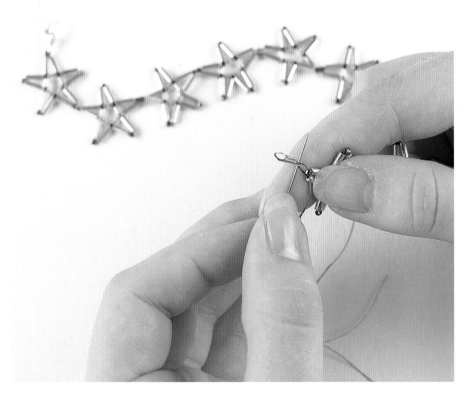

Templates

↑ Embroidered bag (Full size) (pages 46–49)

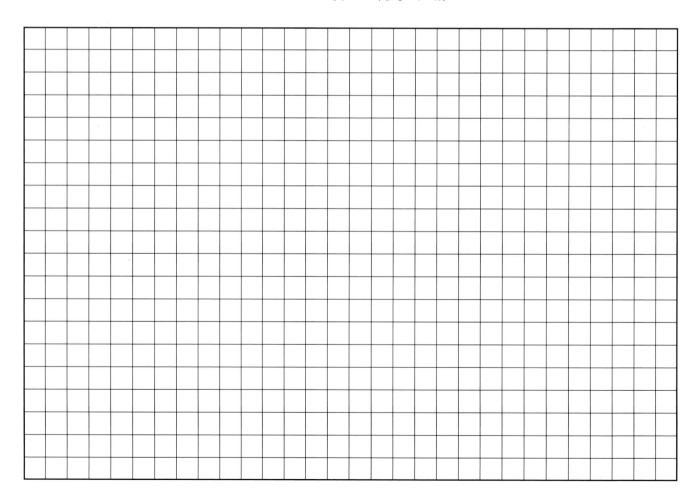

↑ A chart of blank squares for planning your own beadwork designs

Suppliers

USA

Ackfield Manufacturing
www.ackfieldwire.com

Artistic Wire
752 N. Larch Ave.
Elmhurst, IL 60126
(630) 530-7567
www.artisticwire.com

Beadalon
(866) 423-2325
www.beadalon.com

Fireworks
Diamond Tech International
5600-C Airport Blvd.
Tampa, FL 33634
(800) 937-9593
www.dticrafts.com

Fiskars
7811 W. Stewart Ave.
Wausau, WI 54401
(800) 500-4849
www.fiskars.com

Pacific Silverworks
461 E. Main St., Suite 1-A
Ventura, CA 93001
(805) 641-1394
www.pacificsilverworks.com

Paramount Wire Company
2–8 Central Ave.
E. Orange, NJ 07018
(973) 672-0500
www.parawire.com

Plaid Industries
P.O. Box 7600
Norcross, GA 30091
(800) 842-4197
www.plaidonline.com

Pepperell Braiding Company
22 Lowell St.
Pepperell, MA 01463
(800) 343-8114
www.pepperell.com

Pincharming
P.O. Box 037063
Elmont, IL 11003
(800) 566-0531
www.pincharming.com

PMC Connection
(866) 762-2529
www.pmcconnection.com

Prairie Craft Co.
P.O. Box 209
Florissant, CO 90816
(800) 779-0615
www.prairiecraft.com

Rhode Island Bead and Components
15 Industrial Rd.
Cranston, RI 02920
(401) 464-4411
www.ribead.com

Soft Flex Company
P.O. Box 80
Sonoma, CA 95479
(707) 938-3539
www.softflex.com

The Miovi Group
475 James Jackson Ave.
Cary, NC 27513
(919) 388-9822
www.miovi.com

Tools GS
408 St. Paul St.
Rochester, NY 14603
(800) 295-2695
www.toolsgs.com

Westrimcrafts
7855 Hayvenhurst Ave.
Van Nuys, CA 91409
(800) 727-2727
www.westrimcrafts.com

ASSOCIATIONS

USA

American Craft Council
21 S. Eltings Corner Rd.
Highland, NY 12528
(800) 836-3470
www.craftcoucil.com

Arts and Crafts Association of America
4888 Cannon Woods Ct.
Belmont, MI 49306
(616) 874-1721
www.artsandcraftsassoc.com

Association of Crafts & Creative Industries
1100-H Brandywine Blvd.
P.O. Box 3388
Zanesville, OH 43702
(740) 452-4541
www.accicrafts.org

Hobby Industry Association
319 E. 54th St.
Elmwood Park, NJ 07407
(201) 794-1133
www.hobby.org

National Craft Association
1945 E. Ridge Rd., Suite 5178
Rochester, NY 14622
(800) 715-9594

CANADA

Canada Craft and Hobby Association
24 1410-40 Ave., N.E.
Calgary, AL T2E 6L1
(403) 291-0559

Canadian Crafts Federation
c/o Ontario Crafts Council
Designers Walk
170 Bedford Rd., Suite 300
Toronto, ON M5R 2K9
(416) 408-2294
www.canadiancraftsfederation.ca

Index